Level Headers

Find your Power!

written by
Beth Cox

in collaboration with
Power Thoughts founder
Natalie Costa

illustrated by
Vicky Barker

www.bsmall.co.uk

Published by b small publishing ltd. www.bsmall.co.uk © b small publishing ltd. 2019 • 1 2 3 4 5 • ISBN 978-1-911509-97-4
Production: Madeleine Ehm   Publisher: Sam Hutchinson   Editorial: Sam Hutchinson   Design and Art direction: Vicky Barker   Printed in China by WKT Co. Ltd.
All rights reserved. No reproduction, copy or transmission of this publication may be made without written permission. No part of this publication may be reproduced, stored in a retrieval system or transmitted in any form or by any means, electronic, mechanical, photocopying, recording or otherwise, without the prior permission of the publisher.
British Library Cataloguing-in-Publication Data. A catalogue record for this book is available from the British Library.

How this book works

This book is full of activities to help you find your power and overcome nerves. The activities all build on each other so are designed for you to work through in order, but you can skip some and go back if you want, or dip in and out if you'd rather - there are no rules.

Use the icons to find top tips, useful information, suggestions for taking it further, and details of additional resources.

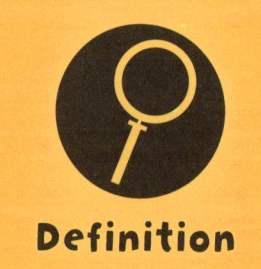

Useful info/fact

Take it further

Top tip

Make your own

Definition

What is your power?

Your power lies in how you feel about yourself inside and how you see your own value in the world. Every single person is important and worthwhile, but sometimes it can be hard to remember that — you forget all the great things you can do and instead focus on what you can't do or what you see as your faults.

Finding your power is about accepting who you are and looking after yourself. Your differences and your quirks make you interesting and make you *you*. When you find your power, it will affect everything you do. You'll feel good about yourself, believe in yourself, and cope better when things don't go as you had hoped or planned.

Contents

4-5	You are a miracle	20-21	Press the button
6-7	Truly awesome	22-23	Self talk
8-9	Create yourself	24-25	Feeling thankful
10-11	Brain power	26-27	A good start
12-13	Find kind	28-29	Deep sleep
14-15	Wake up to your feelings	30-31	Focus and calm
16-17	Big feelings	32	Take it further
18-19	Shake it out		

You are a miracle

The chances of you being born, when you were born and with your specific DNA is roughly 1 in 400 trillion.

These odds don't even take into account the chances of all your ancestors living to be old enough to have children and, each time, the particular cells combining to create the next generation of your particular ancestors. When that is taken into account the odds are one in ... a number too big to fit in this entire book.

Basically the odds of you existing are zero. But here you are. Reading this book. It must be a miracle.

"A miracle is an event so unlikely as to be almost impossible."
— Dr. Ali Binazir

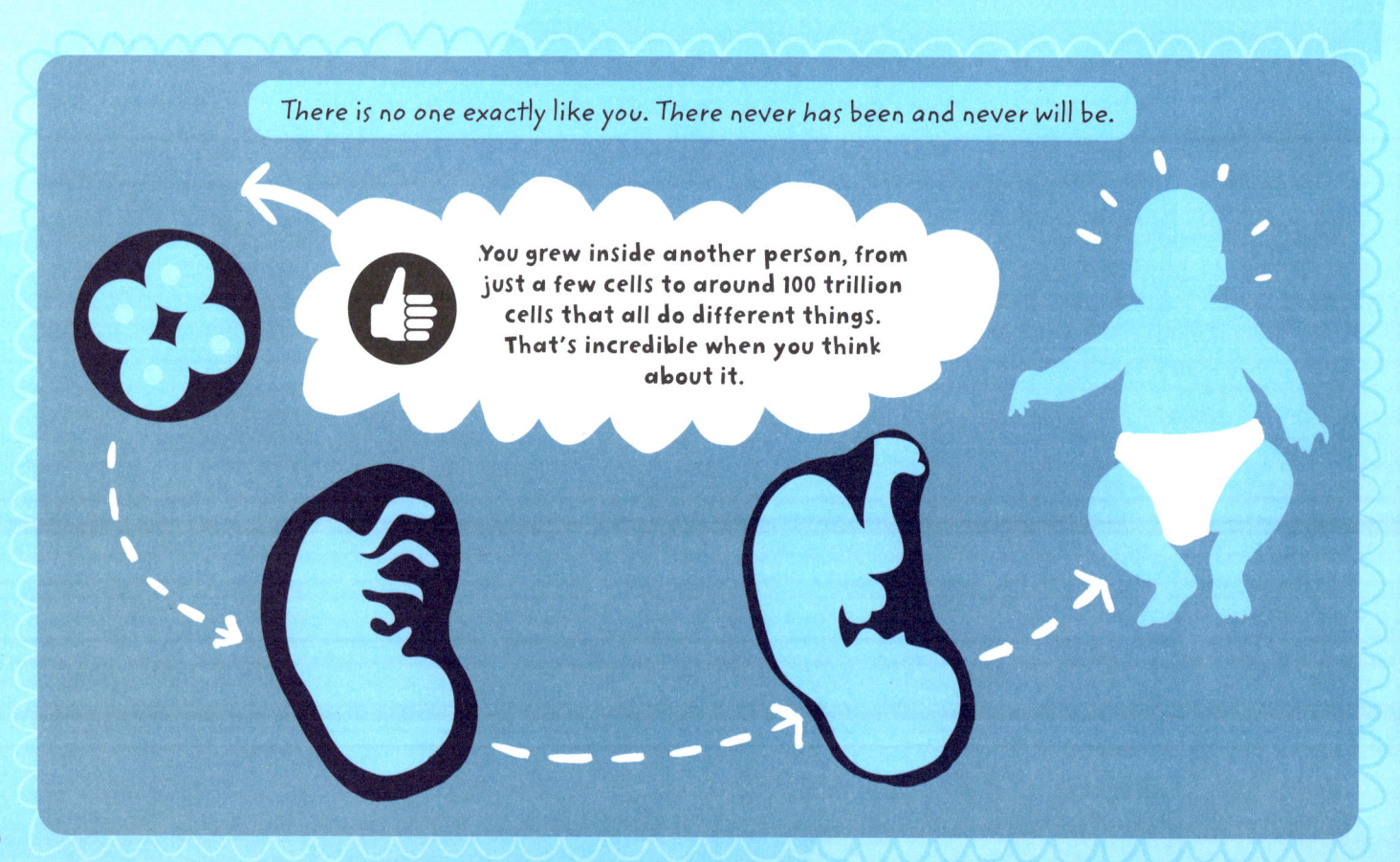

There is no one exactly like you. There never has been and never will be.

You grew inside another person, from just a few cells to around 100 trillion cells that all do different things. That's incredible when you think about it.

My name: Joshua

It means: a savior and a deliverer

Draw or stick a picture of yourself here.

Make a fingerprint here.

Your fingerprints, just like you, are unique. There are no two sets of fingerprints that are the same — even identical twins have different fingerprints.

Even if you don't yet believe that you are a miracle, there are plenty of people who do. These might be people in your family, or people at school…

Write the names of the people who love and care about you. You can draw a picture of them too if you like.

Truly awesome

We use the word 'awesome' all the time, but what does it really mean? Awe is an overwhelming feeling of wonder. Something breathtaking or mind blowing. If we stop and think about the world, and the things we can see and do every day, so much is just incredible. Different things fill different people with wonder.

Awesome: extremely impressive or daunting; inspiring awe.

It might be nature:

A flower growing all its different parts from a tiny seed or a caterpillar transforming into a butterfly with symmetrically patterned wings.

It might be technology:

Being able to find out almost anything on the internet, or talking to someone thousands of miles away and being able to see their face, or humans walking on the moon.

"Look deep into nature, and then you will understand everything better." - Albert Einstein

The average worker bee only lives for five or six weeks and produces only about 1/12th teaspoon of honey in her lifetime.

Beavers have transparent eyelids so they can see underwater with their eyes shut.

The first computer weighed around 27 tonnes. That is more than four elephants!

Spend ten minutes just looking at something in your house or outside and wonder about how it works.

This is awesome!

How did you feel when you thought about how this worked?

How it works

Find out as much as you can about how it works.

Every day, take the time to stop and wonder at something. Keep in touch with how awesome life truly is.

Create yourself

It's easy to think that who you are is fixed. You are the way you are and that's that. But it just isn't true. You get to choose how you act, what you do, how you think about yourself, and even how you feel.

So who do you want to be? You really can choose. Do you want to be brave? Strong? Kind? Helpful? Determined? Confident? Good at science? It's a tricky question. It might be easier to start by thinking about what problems you'd like to solve. Then you can work out what kind of person you need to be and what you will need to do to solve them.

Malala Yousafzai chose to stand up for what she believed in and spoke out about the right to education for girls in Pakistan. She was just one person, but decided that her voice was important.

"You are, in every moment, deciding who and what you are."
- Neale Donald Walsch

I want to solve the problem of so much rubbish going to landfill.

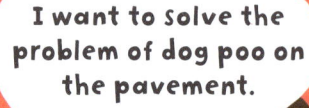

I want to solve the problem of dog poo on the pavement.

I want to solve the problem of homelessness.

Write the problem you want to solve here.

Make a mind map of how you might solve the problem and what you might need to solve it. You can add extra sections, ideas of how you will work on the strengths and skills, and use colours and illustrations. See page 32 for a list of strengths and skills.

Remember to think about who you want to become to solve this problem.

Skills   Strengths

Problem

Ideas   Equipment

There is no right or wrong way to solve any problem — just get creative. You might even need things that haven't been invented yet!

Use a separate piece of paper if you need more space.

Brain power

You are born with around 100 billion neurons (a type of brain cell). As you grow and learn, connections are made between these brain cells. The more you do something, the stronger the connection for that skill in the brain becomes. But if you stop working on a skill, the brain thinks that it is unnecessary so the connection fades away. You have to use it or you lose it.

Your brain changes every day and dealing with challenges makes your brain stronger.

I want to be more adventurous. I'm going to try something new each week.

I want to be more organised. I'm going to tidy up after myself.

"Sitting on your shoulders is the most complicated object in the known universe."
- Michio Kaku

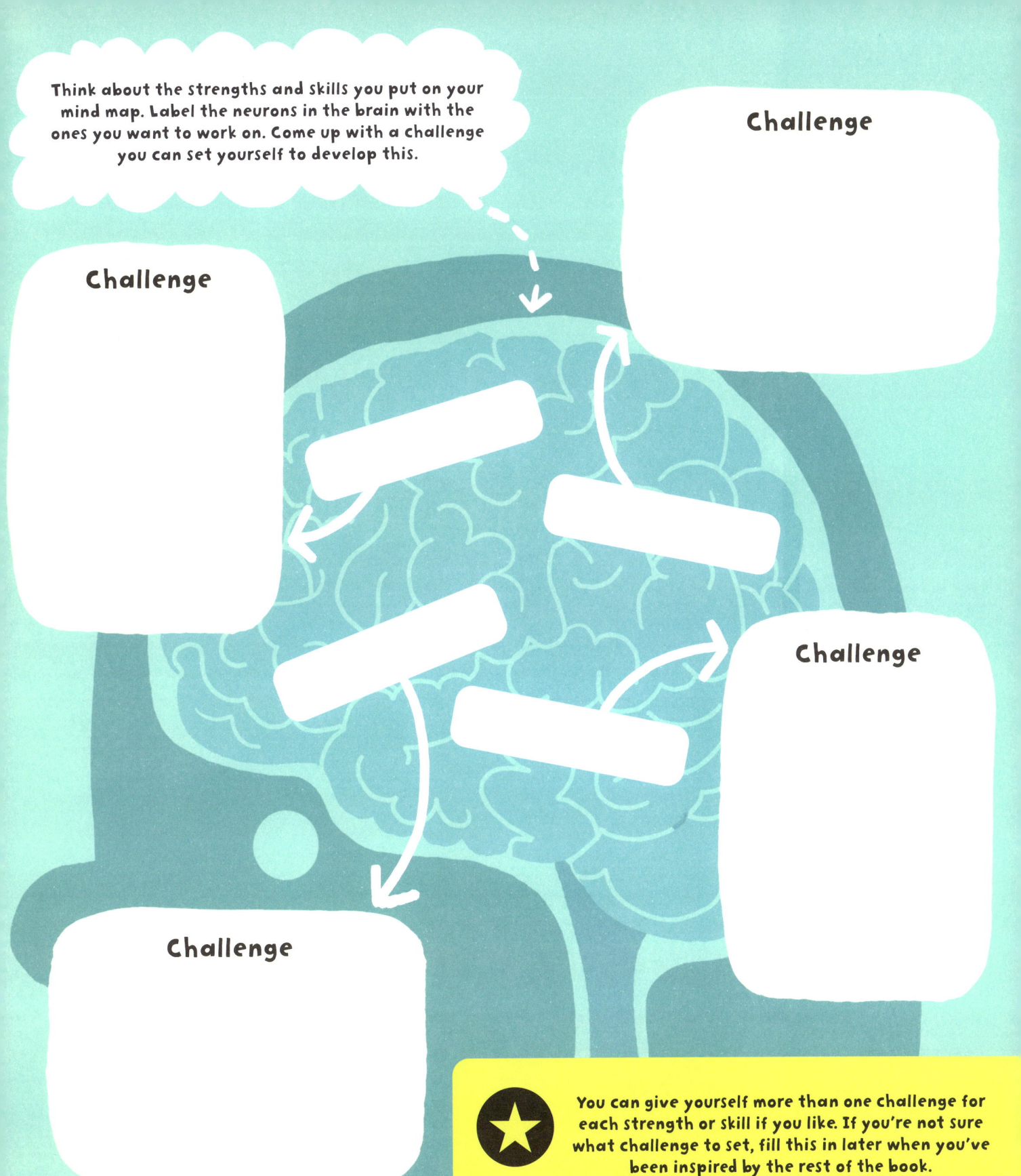

Think about the strengths and skills you put on your mind map. Label the neurons in the brain with the ones you want to work on. Come up with a challenge you can set yourself to develop this.

Challenge

Challenge

Challenge

Challenge

You can give yourself more than one challenge for each strength or skill if you like. If you're not sure what challenge to set, fill this in later when you've been inspired by the rest of the book.

Find kind

Being kind doesn't just make someone else feel good – it will make you feel good too. Being kind makes you happier, more optimistic and gives you more energy. It can help you forget about worries and makes you calmer.

Kindness spreads too: when people see you being kind, they are more likely to do something kind for someone else.

"No act of kindness, no matter how small, is ever wasted."
- Aesop

Colour in the square when you carry out an act of kindness. Why not use a colour that reflects how doing that thing made you feel. You can make up some of your own too.

★ The more random acts of kindness you do, the more natural it will become.

Challenge yourself to carry out one random act of kindness each day. Can you do this for a whole month?

Compliment someone.	Feed the birds.	Pick up litter.
Leave a note in a library book.		Hold the door open.
	Talk to someone new.	Smile at someone.	Read a book to someone.

12

Give someone a flower.	Invite someone to join in.	Write a thank you note.	Offer to help someone.
	Give someone a hug.		Bake a cake to share.
Visit a neighbour.	Tell a joke.	Let someone else go first.	
Wave at people on buses.		Plant a flower.	Tell someone why they are special to you.
Make a get well card.	Help someone carry shopping.	Give up your seat.	Donate unused toys.

Wake up to your feelings

The range of feelings you have is huge. The main ones people talk about are happiness, sadness, anger and fear, but you can feel other feelings too.

Emotions are neither 'good' nor 'bad'. It is fine to feel however you feel. What can be a problem is the reaction to an emotion. To feel angry is okay. But hitting someone because you are angry is not, and will not make anyone feel good, least of all you. It might even make you feel other less pleasant emotions such as shame.

> "Feelings are much like waves, we can't stop them from coming but we can choose which one to surf."
> - Jonatan Mårtensson

👍 It takes less than one and a half minutes for an emotion to be triggered and pass through the body. It is your choice whether you let it go or let it take over. You are in charge.

Feelings

disappointed, annoyed, thrilled, worried, nervous, happy, furious, afraid, calm, overwhelmed, excited, insignificant, content, panicky, miserable, angry, cross, pleased, anxious, gloomy, hopeful, joyful, shy, peaceful, lonely

Choose a feeling and write it in one of the boxes.
- Think about where you feel it in your body and link the box to that area.
- Draw how it feels in your body.
- Use a colour to reflect how that feeling feels.

Keep a record of your feelings over the next week. Where do you feel each one? How long does each feeling last? How does the feeling change?

Big feelings

Some of the less pleasant emotions you experience can become really big and affect your mood. Each emotion is giving you a message so you need to tune in and listen. If you can identify the message, you might be able to find more positive ways of dealing with your big feelings.

"Nothing ever goes away until it teaches us what we need to know."
- Pema Chodron

Overwhelmed
Too much is happening. Sad and scared.
- Avoid everything.
- Focus on one thing at a time.

Angry
Something is in our way. Gives you energy.
- Lash out.
- Find a solution.

👍 Happiness simply tells us to do more of whatever caused that feeling!

1. Close your eyes and think about a big feeling you have. Write the feeling at the top of the box. Does it have a shape or a colour? Try to represent the feeling in the box. Do not think too much about what it looks like, just draw.

2. Causes
What causes this feeling?

3. Messages
What is your feeling trying to tell you? The message might be different depending on the cause.

4. Actions
Now you have worked out the message, think of a more positive way to deal with it.

Shake it out

Sometimes it can seem really hard to change how you feel — especially if you are feeling sad, frustrated or angry. There is nothing wrong with feeling any of those things — but as those feelings may not be pleasant, you probably won't want to stay with them for too long. Moving can change how you feel.

⭐ **Try these things to change your mood.**

Frustrated?
Jump up and down or run on the spot.

Angry?
Let the energy out. You can make a noise or stamp your foot or just run around outside (keep yourself and others safe).

Gloomy?
Put on some music and dance.

⭐ If you're feeling shocked, overwhelmed or excited, you might need calming rather than energetic movement, such as stretching, deep breathing, or rolling your shoulders.

Let's do a quick experiment.

1. Hold up your left hand. Think about how it feels right now. Heavy or light? Tense or relaxed? Choose a coloured pencil or pen and write words to describe how it feels.

2. Set a timer for a minute and shake your left hand until the timer goes. Think about how your hand feels now. Choose a different colour and write all the words you would use to describe it.

"There are shortcuts to happiness, and dancing is one of them."
- Vicki Baum.

Press the button

A TV programme can make you feel happy, amused, worried, anxious, stressed, sad, bored or joyful. If you do not like how something is making you feel you can change the channel just by pressing a button.

You can do the same thing with your mind. You get to choose how you feel. You can focus on the things that feel bad or the ones that feel good.

Draw a scene from your least favourite TV programme.

Imagine watching it. How do you feel?

Draw a scene from your favourite TV programme.

Imagine watching it. How do you feel?

How did your body, posture and thoughts change when you changed the channel? When you are feeling a way you do not like, what could you think instead that would make you feel proud, happy or powerful?

"You and only you are in charge of your feelings."
- Lynne Namka

Self talk

You are in control of your brain — it listens to what you tell it. If you focus on negative things about yourself, your brain will believe you and keep repeating and reinforcing those messages. The good news is that focusing on positive things and things you like about yourself can change your brain pattern and help you feel more positive about yourself.

We call positive statements 'affirmations'. Reading affirmations every day trains your brain to focus on these messages.

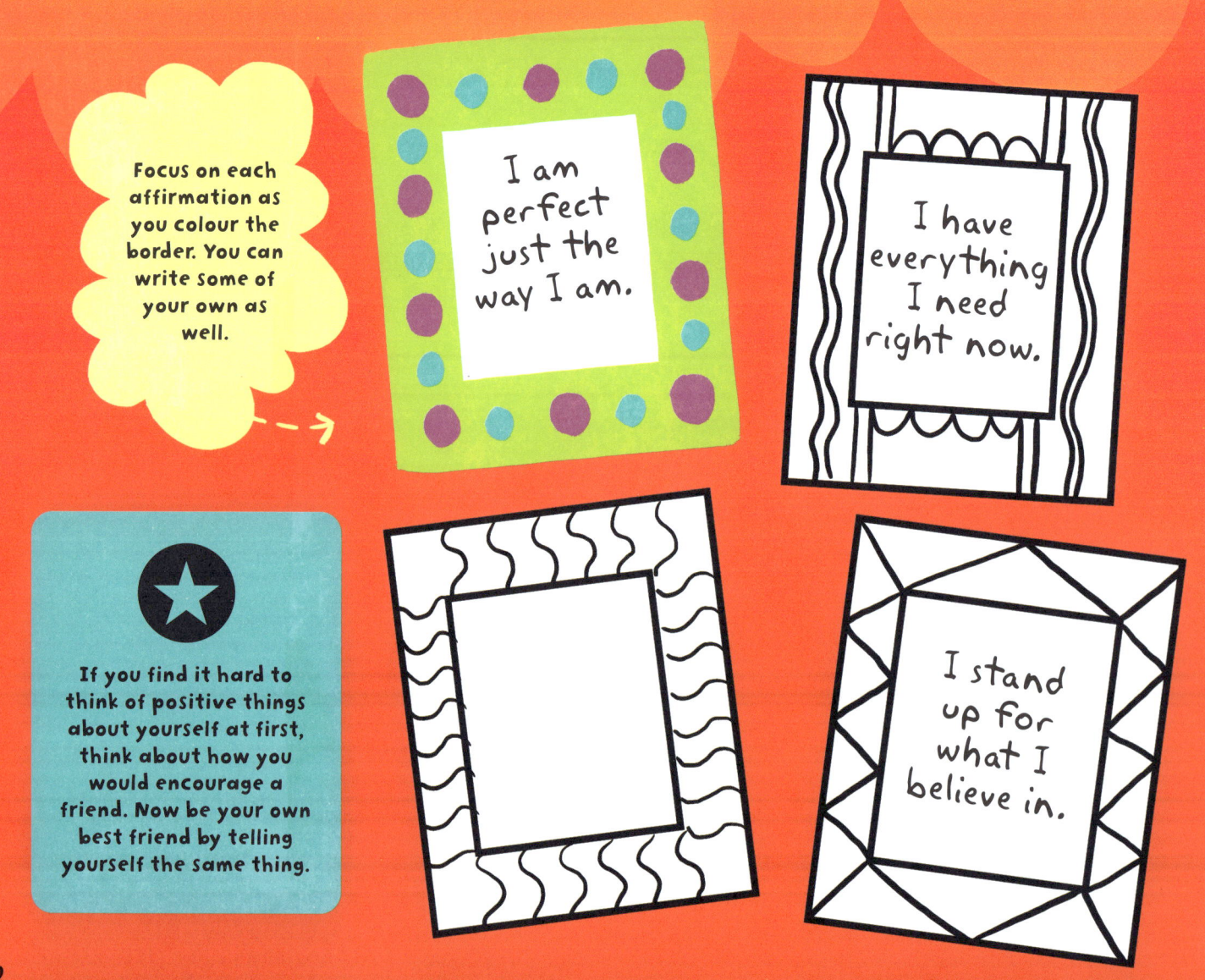

Focus on each affirmation as you colour the border. You can write some of your own as well.

I am perfect just the way I am.

I have everything I need right now.

If you find it hard to think of positive things about yourself at first, think about how you would encourage a friend. Now be your own best friend by telling yourself the same thing.

I stand up for what I believe in.

I believe in myself.

All of my problems have solutions.

You can copy, cut out and display these affirmations somewhere you'll read them regularly.

I learn from my mistakes.

I will not compare myself to others.

I get better with practice.

I am in charge of my feelings.

Make you own affirmation card templates so you can write more.

If you are struggling to think of affirmations, you can look online for inspiration.

23

Feeling thankful

When a bad thing has happened during the day, it is really easy to focus on that and forget about all the good things that happened. By thinking of the things you are grateful for each day you can train your brain to start focusing on the positive instead.

If you find it hard to think of what you are grateful for, start by thinking about what went well for you each day.

We are seven times more likely to notice a negative than a positive.

"Every day may not be good, but there's something good in every day."
- Alice Morse Earle

My toast was the perfect colour this morning.

The sun came out as I walked to school.

My boots kept my feet dry in the rain.

Write three things you are grateful for each day. Even if you have had a really bad day, look hard and you will find something good.

Each gratitude needs to be different. It will not work if you say you are grateful for your lunch every day!

Monday
1. _____
2. _____
3. _____

Tuesday
1. _____
2. _____
3. _____

Wednesday
1. _____
2. _____
3. _____

Thursday
1. _____
2. _____
3. _____

Friday
1. _____
2. _____
3. _____

Saturday
1. _____
2. _____
3. _____

Sunday
1. _____
2. _____
3. _____

Gratitude prompts

weather
food
kindness
shelter
nature
people
learning
health
hobbies
seasons
space
favourites
freedom
adventure
moments
gifts
colours

To really change your brain pattern you need to keep this up for three weeks. Why not find a small book to use as a gratitude journal or make your own template.

A good start

What would be a good start to the day for you? Maybe you need a long time to wake up or maybe you jump out of bed as soon as you open your eyes. How you start the day can affect your mood until you go to bed that night.

Making your bed in the morning is a simple task that gives you a feeling of order and achievement. It also makes it nicer to climb into at bedtime!

Wake up

Think about how you like to be woken up. An alarm, sunlight through the curtains or blinds, a song on the radio, someone talking to you?

"The day will be what you make it, so rise, like the sun, and burn."
- William C. Hannan

Think about how you can shake yourself out of a bad mood on those days when you just wake up in a funk.

Getting ready

Maybe put out your clothes the night before, have a hot or cold shower, take some deep breaths, make the bed!

Plan your morning routine!

Breakfast

What can you eat to make you feel good and give you energy for the day?

Movement

Motivate yourself with movement in the morning. Stretch, dance or jump on the bed!

Power statements

Write three affirmations that you can read to start your day well.

1. ----------------------------------

2. ----------------------------------

3. ----------------------------------

Deep sleep

How much you sleep, where you sleep and how well you sleep has a big impact on how you feel.

Things like bright lights, noise, thoughts whirring through your brain, green light from screens, a busy day, feeling anxious and having too much energy can all stop you sleeping well.

Relaxing and winding down before bed allows you to fall asleep quickly and sleep deeply, meaning you will wake up refreshed.

Bedtime tools

What do you think would work for you?

★ It's best to avoid screens for at least 30 minutes before bed, but the longer the better. Remember to include switching off electronics in your routine.

Plan a bedtime routine to help you sleep better. You might want to start with the time you go to bed and work backwards, but leave space for anything you do once you are in bed, such as reading a book.

What can you do to use up energy before you wind down?

Time	Activity

Write the time you should be in bed here.

Focus and calm

Your brain is busy all the time and this can make you feel busy and buzzing. Taking time to quieten your thoughts or focus on something that does not take too much brainpower can help you feel calmer and more relaxed.

It is estimated that we have between 12,000 and 80,000 thoughts a day, but it could be even more.

Detailed colouring can help you relax and clear your mind. Colour these patterns when you need to relax.

Make your own symmetrical patterns to colour in.

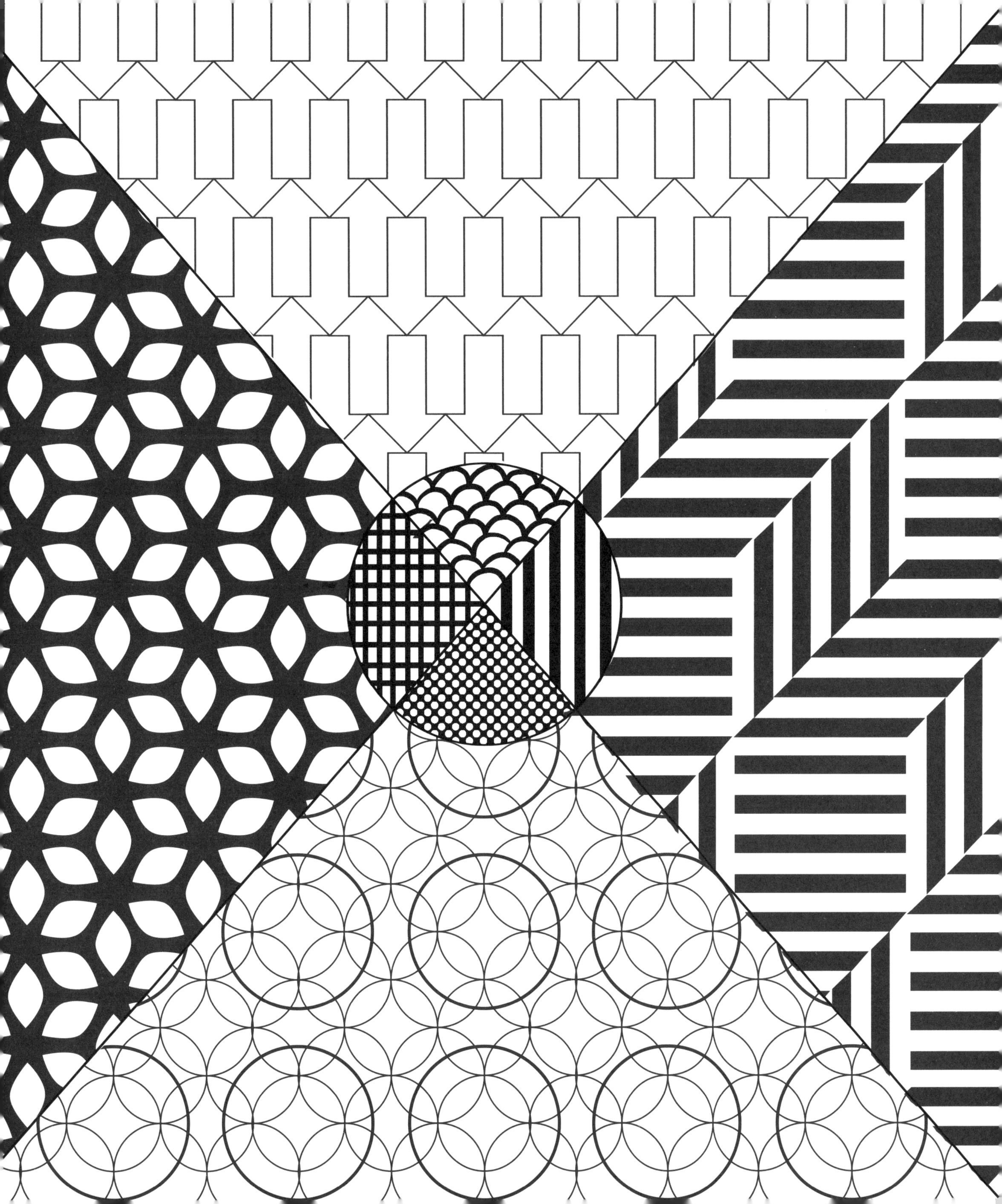

Take it further

Surround yourself with people who make you feel good about yourself.

Look after your body, eat well and keep moving.

Do some yoga.

Take responsibility for something like a plant, a pet or a household task.

Keep your space organised. Mess can make you stressed. Get rid of things you no longer need and find a home for the things you want to keep.

Sit quietly somewhere with your eyes closed for 5 minutes (start with 1 minute if 5 is too hard).

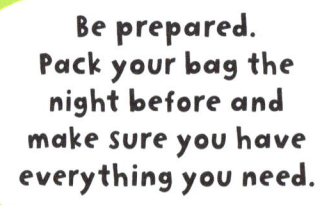

Be prepared. Pack your bag the night before and make sure you have everything you need.

Strengths and skills

* courageous
* creative
* kind
* outspoken
* open-minded
* love of learning
* brave
* honest
* assertive

* energetic
* self control
* ambition
* adventurous
* caring
* communicative
* determined
* empathetic
* organised

* observant
* inventive
* sociable
* thoughtful
* tolerant
* warm
* curious
* efficient
* helpful
* imaginative

* neat
* cautious
* leader
* humourous
* modest
* team player
* critical thinker
* risk taker

* flexible
* hopeful
* able to compromise
* logical
* outgoing
* patient
* persuasive
* practical